For you,
Happy Reading!

ISBN: 9798364370815

Growing Readers

All rights reserved

The Box

T. Paris

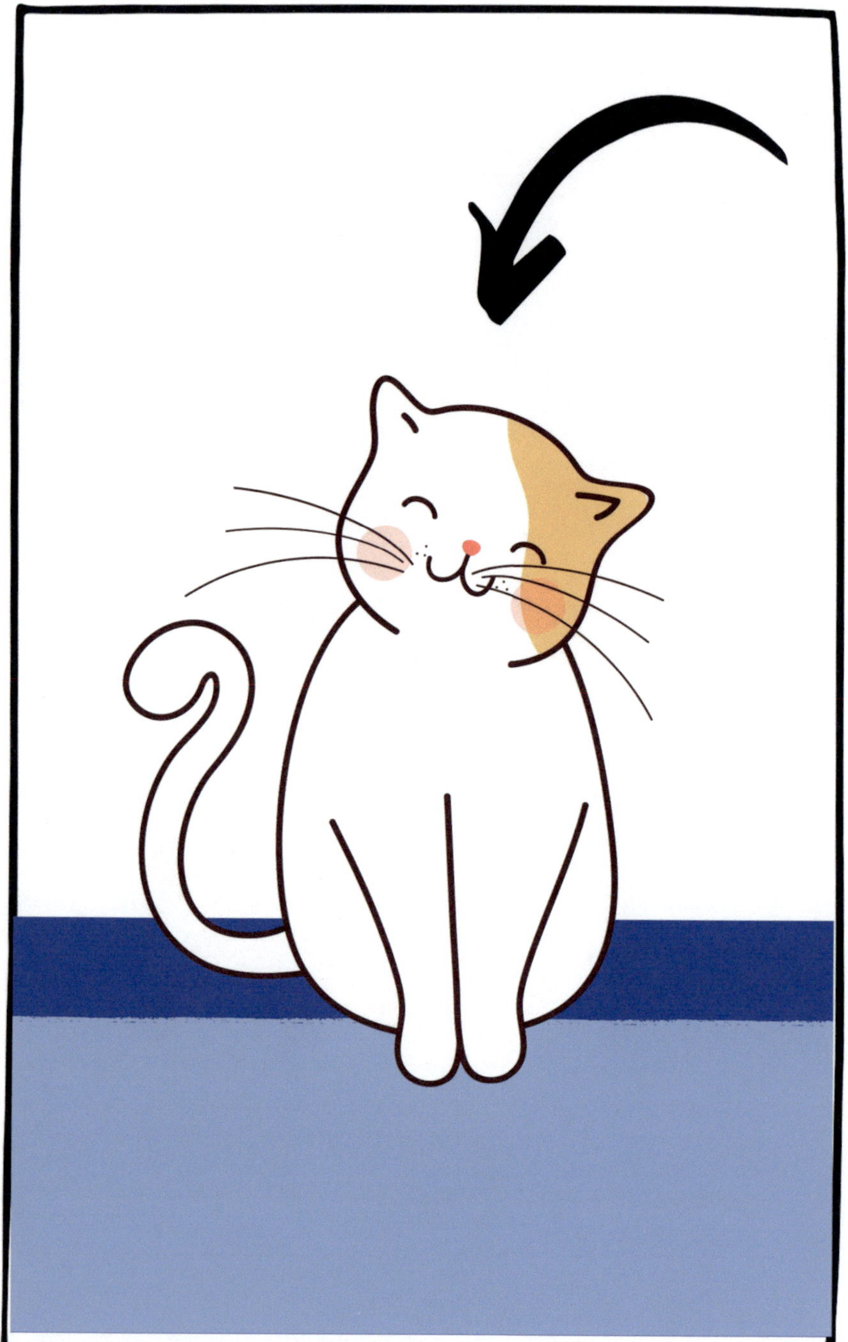

cat

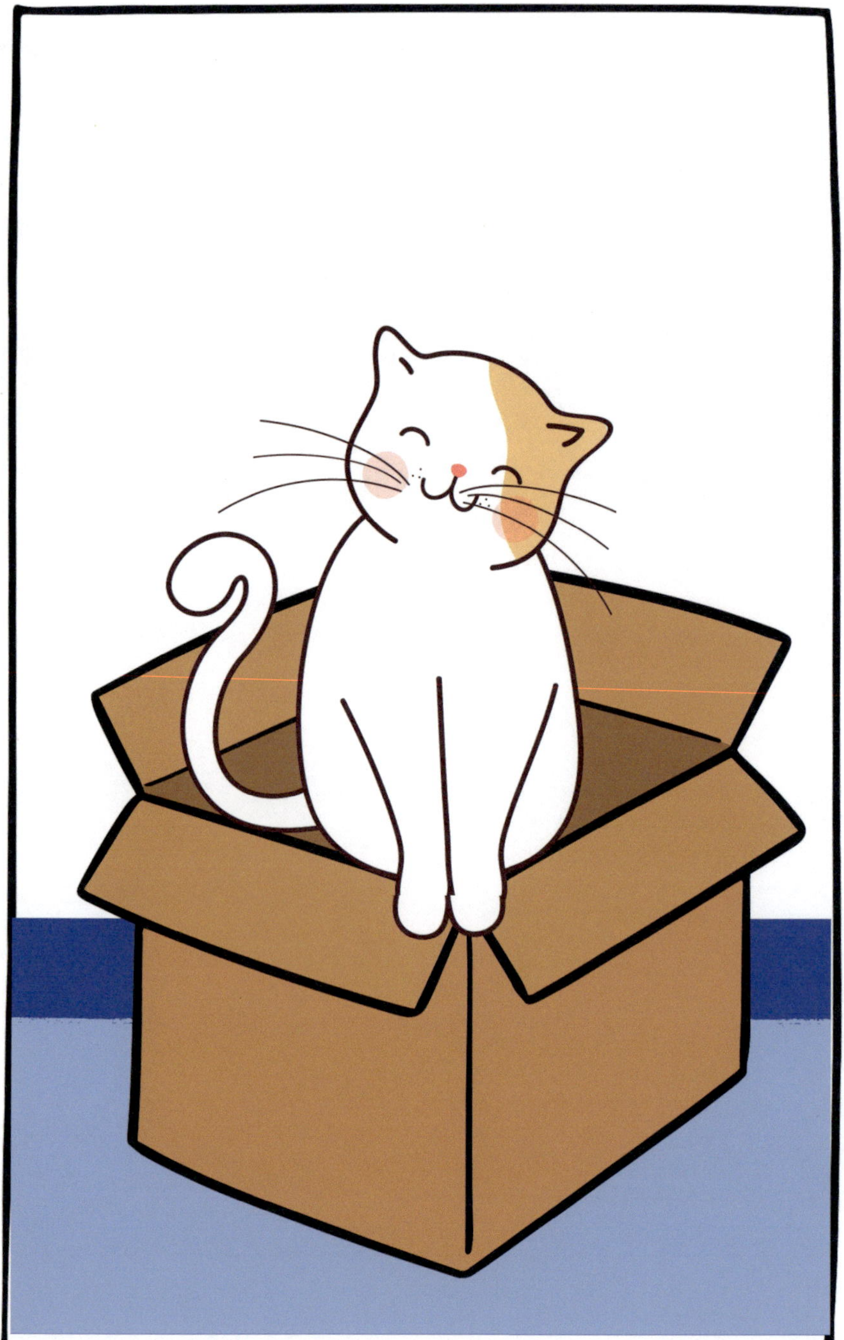

A cat in a box.

6

dog

8

A dog on a box.

10

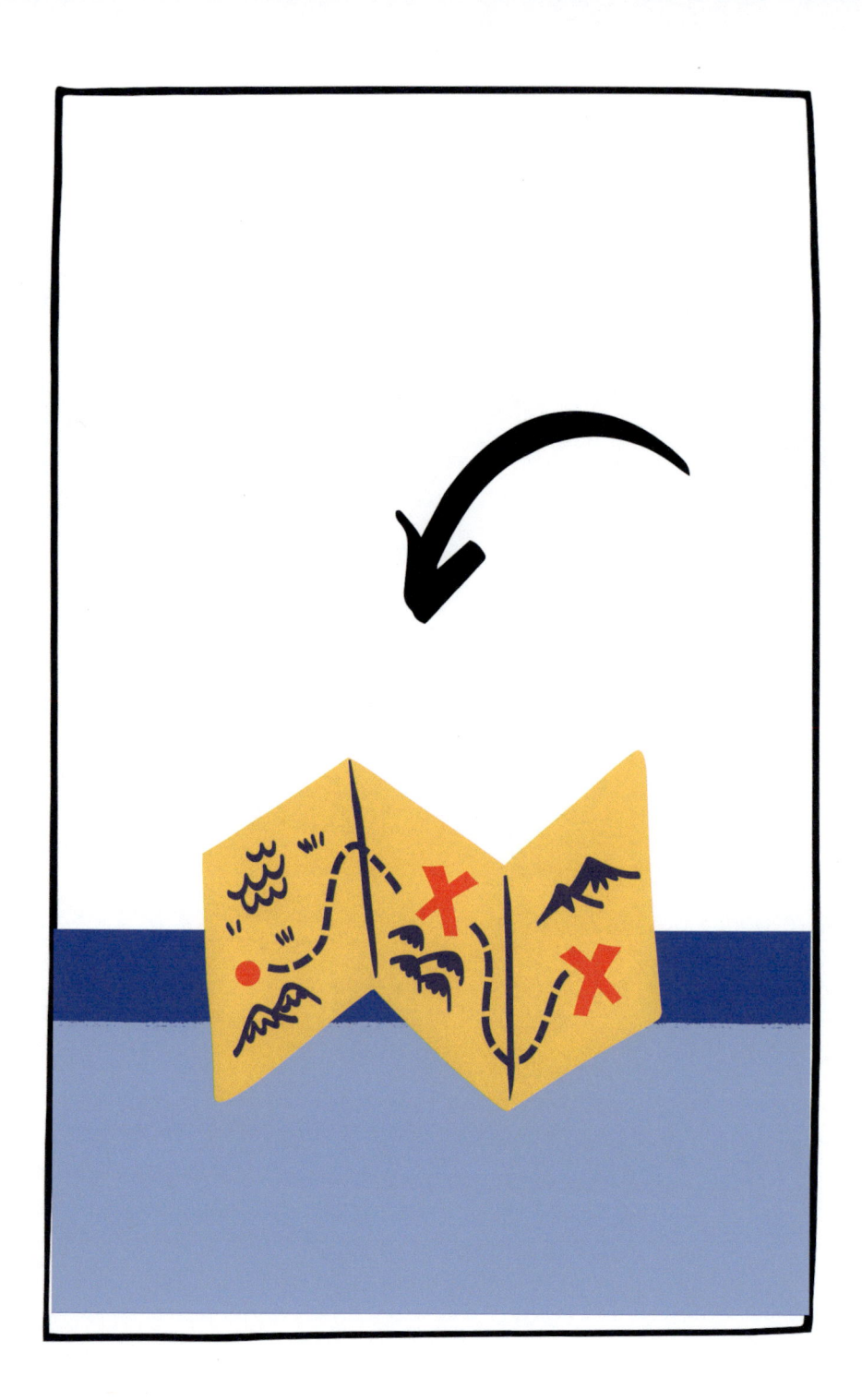

map

12

I see a **map** in a box.

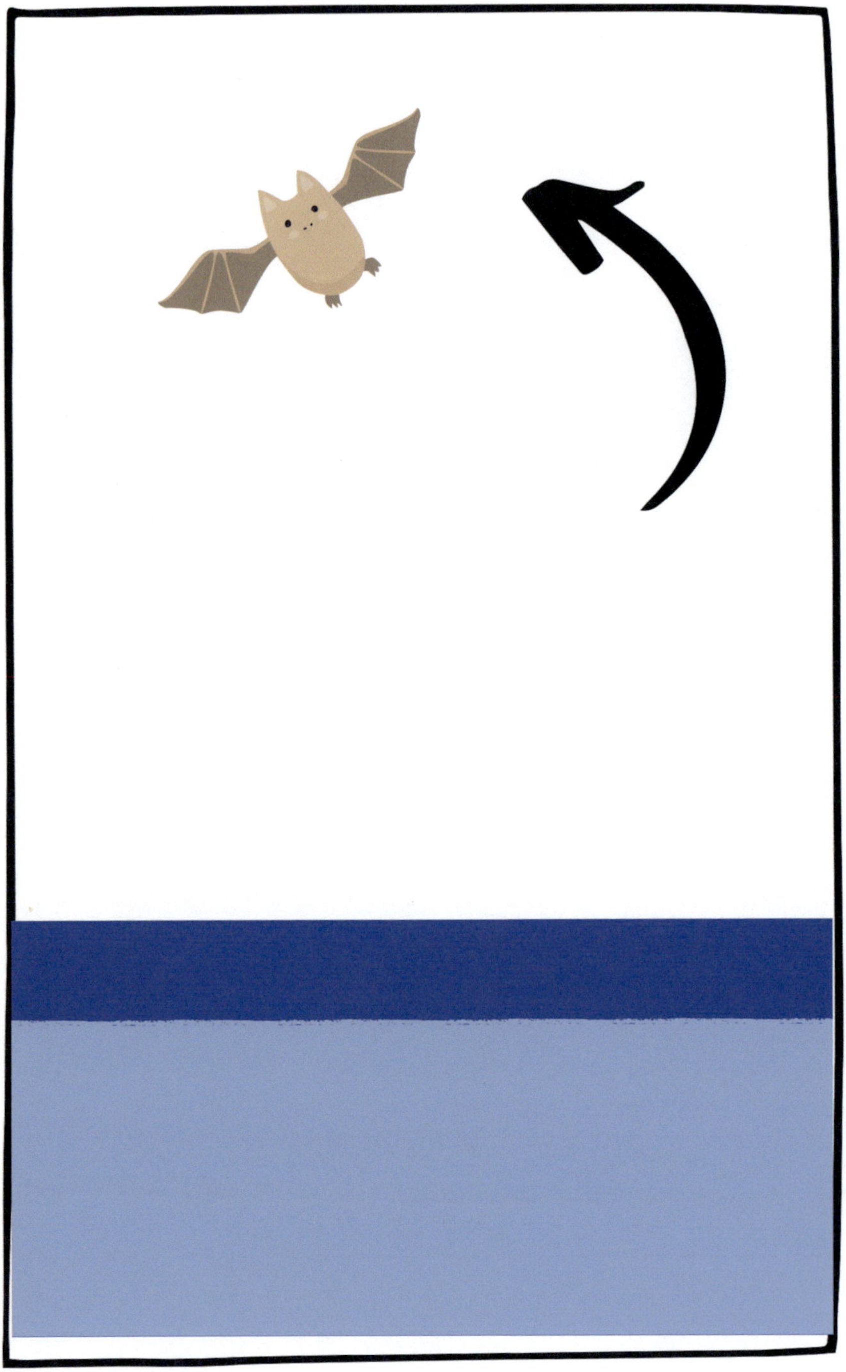

bat

16

A bat in a box?
No, no, no.
Go, bat, go!

18

me

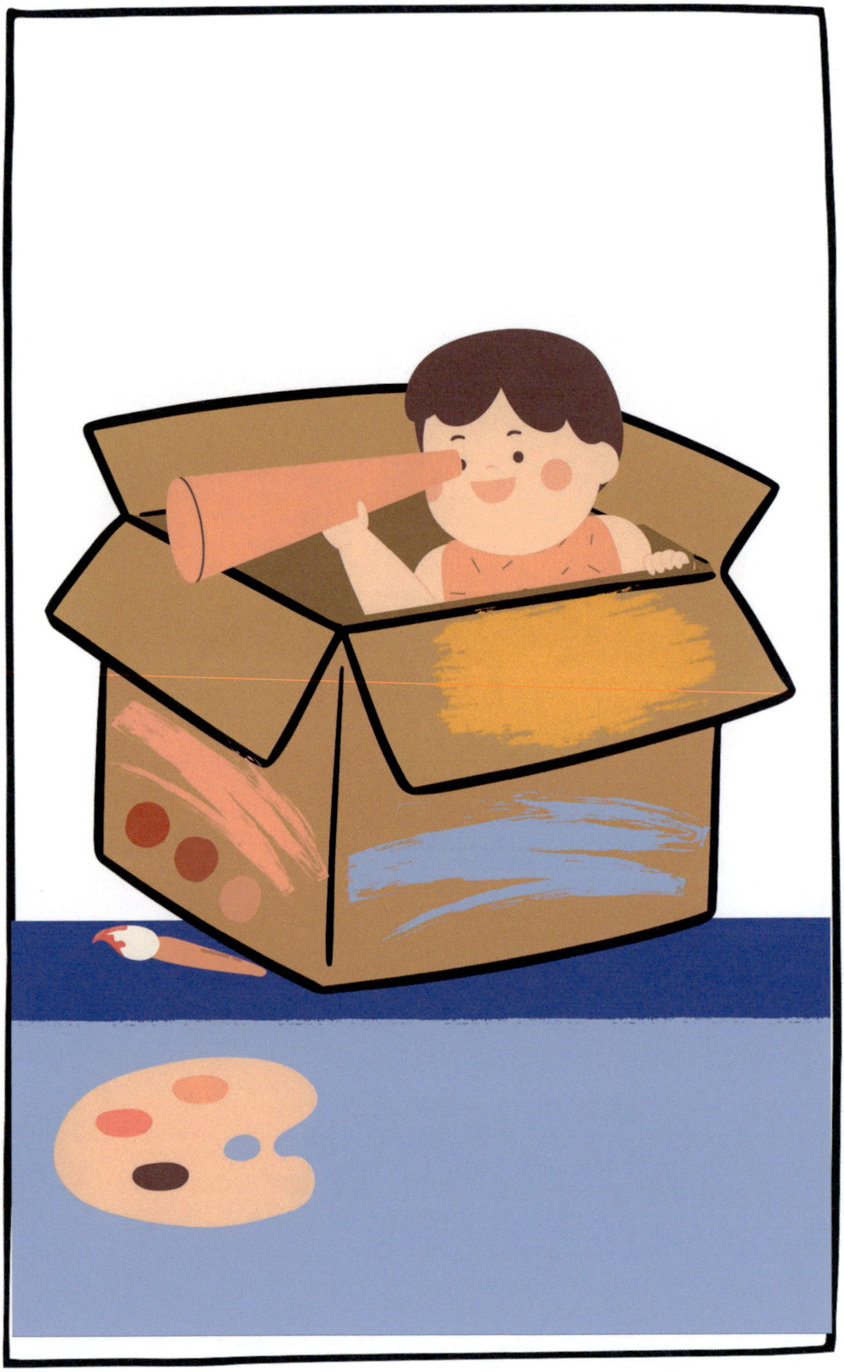

I am in a box!

Made in the USA
Columbia, SC
05 March 2024